LET'S FIND OUT! SOCIAL STUDIES SKILLS

HOW DO YOU READ CHARTS AND GRAPHS?

LAURA LORIA

Britannica®
Educational Publishing

IN ASSOCIATION WITH

ROSEN
EDUCATIONAL SERVICES

Published in 2019 by Britannica Educational Publishing (a trademark of Encyclopædia Britannica, Inc.) in association with The Rosen Publishing Group, Inc.
29 East 21st Street, New York, NY 10010

Distributed exclusively by Rosen Publishing.
To see additional Britannica Educational Publishing titles, go to rosenpublishing.com.

First Edition

Britannica Educational Publishing
J.E. Luebering: Executive Director, Core Editorial
Mary Rose McCudden: Editor, Britannica Student Encyclopedia

Rosen Publishing
Jane Katirgis: Editor
Nelson Sá: Art Director
Brian Garvey: Designer
Ellina Litmanovich: Book Layout
Cindy Reiman: Photography Manager
Karen Huang: Photo Researcher

Library of Congress Cataloging-in-Publication Data

Names: Loria, Laura, author.
Title: How do you read charts and graphs? / Laura Loria.
Description: New York : Britannica Educational Publishing, in Association with Rosen Educational Services, 2019 | Series: Let's find out! Social studies skills | Audience: Grades 1-5. | Includes bibliographical references and index.
Identifiers: LCCN 2018013666| ISBN 9781508107002 (library bound) | ISBN 9781508107194 (pbk.) | ISBN 9781508107354 (6 pack)
Subjects: LCSH: Social sciences—Charts, diagrams, etc—Juvenile literature. | Statistics--Juvenile literature. | Charts, diagrams, etc—Juvenile literature.
Classification: LCC HA31 .L5975 2018 | DDC 300.2/1—dc23
LC record available at https://lccn.loc.gov/2018013666

Manufactured in the United States of America

Photo credits: Cover, back cover, p. 1 and interior pages background Thanakorn Phanthura/EyeEm/Getty Images; p. 4 Ulrike Schmitt-Hartmann/The Image Bank/Getty Images; p. 5 pictafolio/E+/Getty Images; p. 6 Wanwisspaul/Shutterstock.com; pp. 7, 10, 12, 16 © Encyclopædia Britannica, Inc.; p. 8 Steve Debenport/E+/Getty Images; p. 11 JGI/Jamie Grill/Blend Images/Getty Images; p. 13 Blend Images - KidStock/Brand X Pictures/Getty Images; p. 14 Sean K/Shutterstock.com; p. 15 Hero Images /Getty Images; p. 17 kali9/E+/Getty Images; p. 21 Happy Together/Shutterstock.com; p. 23 Arthimedes/Shutterstock.com; p. 26 Karen Huang; p. 27 Joe Raedle/Getty Images; p. 28 ojal/Shutterstock.com; p. 29 Tetra Images – Rob Lewine/Brand X Pictures /Getty Images.

CONTENTS

ATTENTION GETTERS

When you want to learn about something, you might choose a library book or look online. When you are looking at your choices, what catches your eye? For many people, a page filled with words does not seem very interesting. However, when there are pictures mixed with the words, the page suddenly seems more appealing.

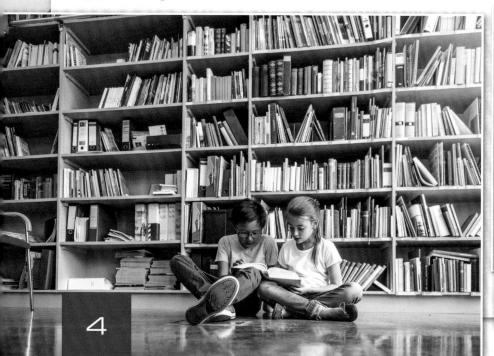

Images like charts and graphs, placed near text in a book, can make a topic easier to understand.

4

You may have heard this saying: "A picture is worth a thousand words." It means that pictures can give a lot of information quickly. Charts and graphs are drawings that do just that. A chart shows information, usually in rows and columns. A graph shows how one type of information relates to another. Both charts and graphs can be very useful. They use colors, numbers, shapes, and some words to make **data** come alive.

When you flip through a book, charts and graphs grab your attention.

CHARTS VS. GRAPHS

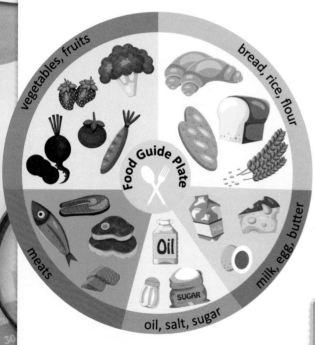

vegetables, fruits

bread, rice, flour

Food Guide Plate

Oil

SUGAR

meats

oil, salt, sugar

milk, egg, butter

Charts and graphs are similar. They are visual displays of data. You can learn a lot about a topic just by noticing things in a picture. Perhaps you notice how large one object is compared to another. Charts are useful for comparing two or more types of things. Graphs can be used to compare things or to show how things change over time.

This graph shows types of food and how much of them people should eat.

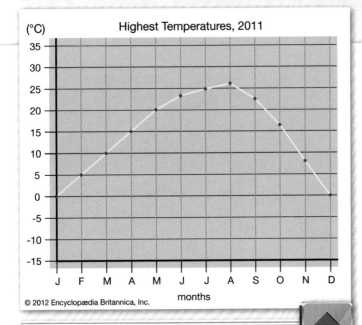

Highest Temperatures, 2011

(°C)

35
30
25
20
15
10
5
0
-5
-10
-15

J F M A M J J A S O N D

months

© 2012 Encyclopædia Britannica, Inc.

The curve of this graph shows how temperatures rose and fell over one year.

COMPARE AND CONTRAST

What are some things that you could show with a chart? What are some things that you could show with a graph?

Every chart or graph has the same basic parts. It has a title, to tell you what the subject is. It has two or more categories, sometimes called variables. Most important, a chart or graph always has data. The data is the information that is shown in picture form. The pictures of data help you to understand the message that the chart or graph is trying to send.

TALLY CHARTS

A very simple type of chart is called a tally chart. Children usually learn how to make this type of chart first. The purpose of a tally chart is to show how many times something happens, or how much of something you have. For example, a tally

Tally charts are a great way to keep score when playing a game with friends.

THINK ABOUT IT

In what other ways could you use a tally chart?

chart can be used to track votes or to count lunch orders at school.

A tally chart has one or more rows or columns. In each row or column, a line called a tally mark represents one thing. To make a tally chart, draw one vertical line for each thing you count. After you draw four lines, if there is a fifth thing to count, draw the fifth line diagonally. This diagonal line crosses over the group of four vertical lines.

The fifth tally mark is drawn at an angle, to show clearly a group of five marks.

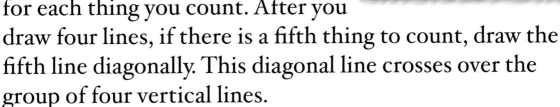

Keeping tally marks in groups of five is useful. When you are done making your tally chart, you can quickly count by fives to get the total.

TABLES

A table is a type of chart that simply shows information as it is. It doesn't always compare things, and sometimes it doesn't even have numbers. Its purpose is to give information quickly, in an easy-to-read way.

Like tally charts, tables have columns and rows to organize information. A table of contents is a good example. This type of table

Some figures of Egyptian mythology	
name	description
Amon	one of the chief gods
Bastet	goddess of music and pregnant women; cat-headed
Hathor	goddess of women and love; cow-headed
Horus	god whose eyes were the Sun and the Moon; appeared as a falcon
Isis	important goddess; wife of Osiris and mother of Horu
Khnum	god of fertility; ram-headed
Mont	god of war; falcon-headed
Nut	goddess of the sky
Osiris	important god of the underworld
Re	chief Sun god
Seth	god of disorder; had some features of a dog
Thoth	god of the Moon, wisdom, and writing; ibis-headed

This table makes it easy to locate information about each god or goddess.

In a table, you find information by looking down and then across.

lists chapter titles for a book in a column on the left. In a column on the right, it lists the **corresponding** page number. A table is a simple way to show information without using unnecessary words.

Imagine how a table of contents would look in complete sentences. In this book, the first line might say, "Chapter One, Attention Getters, can be found on page 4." It is much simpler to put "Attention Getters" in the left column and "4" in the right column. Like other tables, a table of contents makes it easier to find the information you want.

> **VOCABULARY**
> **Corresponding** means matching up.

BAR GRAPHS

Most charts and graphs use as few words as possible. Our brains can understand pictures right away. Words take a bit more time. On a bar graph, a block shape called a bar shows how much of something there is. To compare amounts of different things, a bar graph uses bars of different sizes.

The shape of a bar graph itself is a rectangle. At the top of the rectangle is a title explaining the subject of the graph. On the left side of the rectangle are numbers,

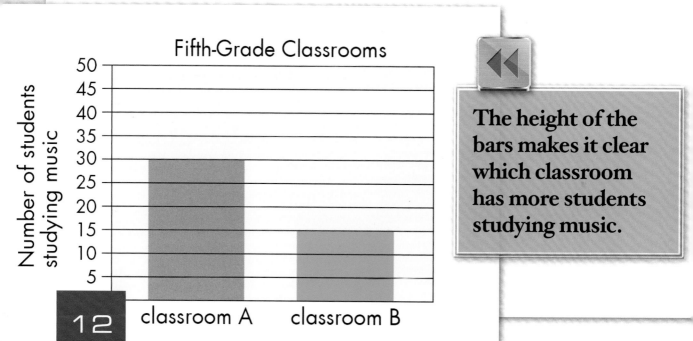

Fifth-Grade Classrooms

Number of students studying music

50
45
40
35
30
25
20
15
10
5

classroom A   classroom B

The height of the bars makes it clear which classroom has more students studying music.

starting at zero and going up. These numbers might go up by ones, twos, fives, tens, or more, depending on how much data there is. A label by these numbers explains what they are counting.

With the information from the bar graph, you know that more music students are in classroom A than classroom B.

COMPARE AND CONTRAST

How is a bar graph similar to a table? How is it different?

The use of colors makes bar graphs easier to read. Shading or patterns also can be used.

The bottom side of the rectangle is where the bars start. Labels on this side name the things that the bars represent. Above these labels are the bars. They can be thick or thin, depending on how much room there is. Often, bars are in different colors to make it easy to tell them apart. The height of each bar lines up with a number on the side of the bar graph. This number is the quantity or size of the thing shown by the bar. A taller bar represents a larger quantity than a shorter bar.

Bar graphs often are used to show the results of polls. In a poll, people are asked a question and given several choices for their answer. Imagine you are taking a poll about what fruit people like best. You ask thirty people if they prefer bananas, apples, or grapes. Then make a bar graph to show the answers. The title of your graph could be "Favorite Fruits." The label on the left side would say "number of people" and could run from zero to thirty. Three bars in different colors would represent the three fruits. At the bottom of each bar would be a label. The labels would say "bananas," "apples," and "grapes." The height of each bar would show how many people preferred that fruit.

Bar graphs can show the results of votes clearly. The heights of the bars make the winning vote obvious.

THINK ABOUT IT

What other types of information can bar graphs show?

CIRCLE GRAPHS

Circle graphs look like their name—they are round in shape. Their purpose is to show differences within a group. The circle is divided into sections. These sections, or "slices," show how much of the whole is represented by each part.

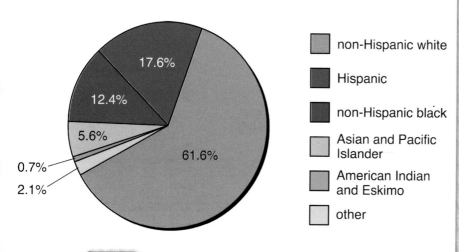

Population by race and Hispanic origin (2015)

17.6%
12.4%
5.6%
0.7%
2.1%
61.6%

- non-Hispanic white
- Hispanic
- non-Hispanic black
- Asian and Pacific Islander
- American Indian and Eskimo
- other

Compare a circle graph with a pizza—the largest slice is the biggest share of the whole.

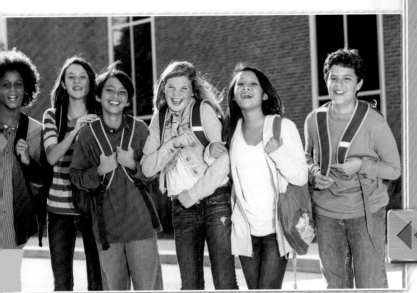

If three of these students choose pizza and three choose hot dogs, a circle graph of their choices will have two equal sections.

Above a circle graph is the title, explaining the subject of the graph. One or more lines separate the circle into sections. Each section has its own color, shading, or pattern. Those differences make it easier to tell the sections apart. Finally, there is a key on the side. The key shows a **sample** of each color, shade, or pattern in the graph. A description next to each sample explains what it means.

VOCABULARY

A **sample** is something that represents a larger thing, often to show what the larger thing is like.

To understand a pie chart, you need to understand fractions and what they mean. A circle graph split into two equal sections shows that each part represents one half of the whole. Of course, most sets of data don't contain two equal parts. In most circle graphs, the sizes of the "slices" show that some amounts are larger than others.

Circle graphs are great for showing differences in a big group. For example, let's say you want to know how many students in your school play video games. The circle would represent all the kids in

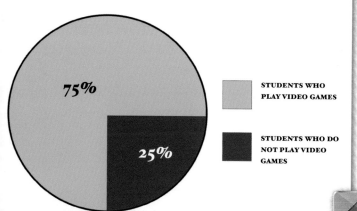

VIDEO GAME PLAYING IN MY SCHOOL

75%

25%

STUDENTS WHO PLAY VIDEO GAMES

STUDENTS WHO DO NOT PLAY VIDEO GAMES

Circle graphs show proportions, or how much of the whole is taken up by a single category.

A circle graph can be used to show election results. In the 2016 presidential election, the Democratic Party and Republican Party got most of the total votes. Other smaller parties, such as the Green Party and the Libertarian Party, got fewer votes.

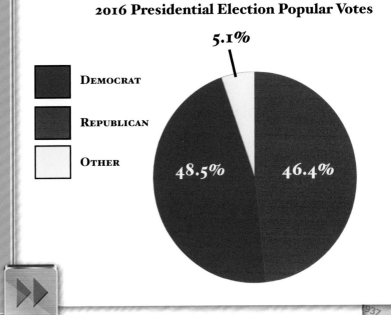

2016 Presidential Election Popular Votes

5.1%

DEMOCRAT

REPUBLICAN

OTHER

48.5%   46.4%

your school. It would be divided into two sections: one for students who play, and one for students who don't. If more than half of the students play video games, that section would take up more than half of the circle.

Another example is a circle graph showing membership in political parties. In the United States, the graph would contain two large sections for the two major parties (Democrats and Republicans). The graph also would have several smaller "slices" for the minor parties.

LINE GRAPHS

Line graphs are one of the trickier graphs to read. Like a bar in a bar graph, a line in a line graph has a height, which represents a quantity. However, the line can change in height as it crosses the graph. The height changes because the line is connecting different points

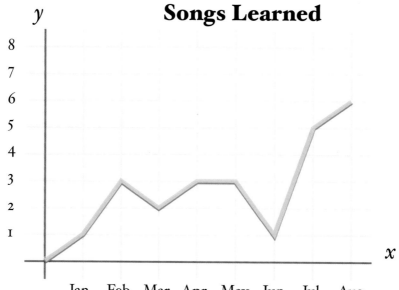

A line graph can help you track your progress when you are learning or training for an activity.

of data. In this way, line graphs show how something changes in value. The change can be over time, or as something else happens.

A line graph is rectangular in shape and contains a grid. The bottom side of the grid often shows the amount of time, in hours, days, months, or years. This side is called the *x*-axis. The left side of the rectangle has a series of numbers, starting at zero and going up. The numbers can increase by ones, fives, tens, or other amounts. The way the numbers increase is called the scale. This side of the graph is called the *y*-axis.

A violin student could use a line graph to keep track of her progress in learning new songs during a year.

THINK ABOUT IT

How is it useful to know how things have changed over a period of time?

For example, a line graph could show how the world's **population** has changed over the last hundred years. The *y*-axis would show numbers up to 8 billion, increasing by steps of one billion. The *x*-axis would show periods of ten years, starting at 1920 and ending in 2020.

Imagine you are putting data on that graph. First, find the year on the x-axis. Then find the number of people on the y-axis. Next, draw imaginary lines up from the x-axis and across

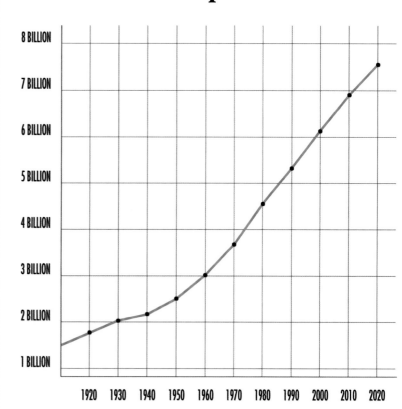

World Population

This map of the world is made up of people. Earth's population is not this evenly spread out, but the map is still a good a reminder of the growing population.

from the y-axis until the lines meet. At that point on the grid, draw a dot. Repeat those steps for each of the years. Finally, connect the dots to make a line.

The direction of the line tells you if quantities have gone up, gone down, or stayed the same. In this example, because the world's population has grown, the line would be heading up as it crossed the grid.

The line shows the rise of the world population over the last century.

VENN DIAGRAMS

An interesting type of chart is a Venn diagram. It shows how groups of things are similar and how they are different. A Venn diagram is made of circles that partly overlap. The overlap creates a shared section between the circles. The shared section contains things that the groups have in common. The parts of the circles that don't overlap contain the differences.

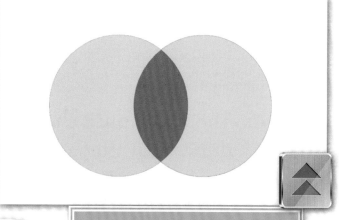

COMPARE AND CONTRAST

How are Venn diagrams and circle graphs similar? How are they different?

The circles in a Venn diagram show what is included and what is left out of a category.

24

A Venn diagram could be used to compare two countries—for example, the United States of America and Mexico. To create this diagram, first you would draw two overlapping circles, one for each country. In the sections that did not overlap, you would write some differences, like languages, population, or holidays. In the shared section of the diagram, you would write similarities. For example, both countries are located in North America, were settled by Europeans, and have a government with three branches.

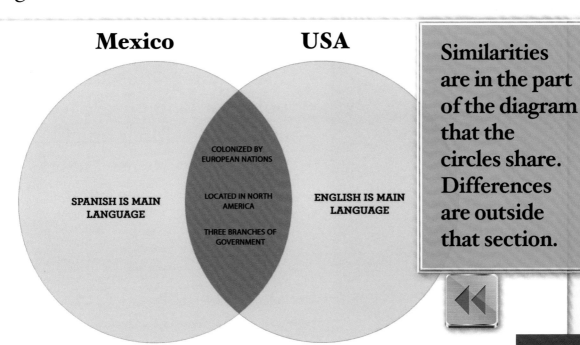

Mexico   **USA**

SPANISH IS MAIN LANGUAGE

COLONIZED BY EUROPEAN NATIONS

LOCATED IN NORTH AMERICA

THREE BRANCHES OF GOVERNMENT

ENGLISH IS MAIN LANGUAGE

Similarities are in the part of the diagram that the circles share. Differences are outside that section.

Charts and Graphs in Everyday Life

You can find charts and graphs in many places. These visual displays can show a lot of information in an easy-to-read way. Charts and graphs are useful tools that help people to understand things quickly.

Restaurants use charts to help you decide what to

Computers can make very precise graphs. Computer-drawn graphs are useful for showing large amounts of data.

It is easier to make choices from a large menu when items and prices are shown clearly, as on this chart.

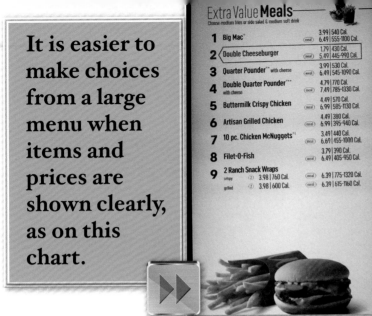

order. In a fast-food restaurant, the menu board often displays items in a table. On the left side, the types of food are listed. On the right is the price of each item. At restaurants where a server takes your order, menus can be set up in a similar way. Menus even can be divided into different charts: one for main meals, one for side dishes or appetizers, and one for desserts.

THINK ABOUT IT

Where have you seen a chart or graph recently?

With a quick glance at this weather chart, you can plan your activities for the week.

Weather reports use charts and graphs to tell us what it's going to be like outside. They might list the day in one column and the temperature in another. More detailed charts might show you the temperature prediction for each hour of the day. Weather forecasters sometimes use line graphs to show how the weather has changed over time. They also use bar charts to compare high and low temperatures.

When you have a medical checkup, a doctor or nurse measures your height and weight. The doctor or nurse then

COMPARE AND CONTRAST

Which type of chart or graph do you think is the easiest to understand? Which type is the hardest?

compares these values to a growth chart. A growth chart is a line graph that shows average growth data for children. The y-axis shows height and weight, and the x-axis shows age. Doctors and nurses use growth charts to find the average height and weight of children at different ages. This information helps them to make sure that children are growing properly.

Tracking your height and weight over time helps doctors to know that you are healthy.

GLOSSARY

column A vertical arrangement of items.

compare To examine in order to discover likenesses or differences.

grid A network of horizontal and vertical lines used for locating points.

horizontal Going side to side across a surface.

key Something that provides an explanation or a way to identify.

poll Questions used to obtain information or opinions from people.

prediction A guess based on some known information.

quantity Amount.

represent To stand for something.

row A horizontal arrangement of items.

scale An arrangement of numbers, often in order from lowest to highest, where the numbers are separated by equal amounts.

tally mark A line marked on a tally chart.

variable A category, group, or factor in a graph.

vertical Going straight up and down from a level surface.

FOR MORE INFORMATION

Books

Edgar, Sherra G. *Bar Graphs* (21st Century Basic Skills Library: Let's Make Graphs). Ann Arbor, MI: Cherry Lake Publishing, 2014.

Edgar, Sherra G. *Pie Graphs* (21st Century Basic Skills Library: Let's Make Graphs). Ann Arbor, MI: Cherry Lake Publishing, 2014.

Flatt, Lizann. *Collecting Data* (Get Graphing! Building Data Literacy Skills). New York, NY: Crabtree Publishing Company, 2017.

Flatt, Lizann. *Line Graphs* (Get Graphing! Building Data Literacy Skills). New York, NY: Crabtree Publishing Company, 2017.

Gosman, Gillian. *Graph It: Reading Charts and Graphs.* New York, NY: PowerKids Press, 2015.

Sikkens, Crystal. *Bar Graphs* (Get Graphing! Building Data Literacy Skills). New York, NY: Crabtree Publishing Company, 2017.

Whyte, Elizabeth. *Making Tally Charts* (Graph It!). New York, NY: Gareth Stevens Publishing, 2015.

Websites

Kids' Zone: Create a Graph
https://nces.ed.gov/nceskids/createagraph/

Math Games: Graphing
https://www.mathgames.com/graphing

Science Sparks: LEGO Bar Charts
http://www.science-sparks.com/lego-bar-charts

INDEX